The Myth
of the
Bad Lord Byron

by

Anne Fleming

The Myth of the Bad Lord Byron
ISBN 0 9513010 2 0

First published 1998 by

Old Forge Press
South Street
Cuckfield
West Sussex
RH17 5LB
Tel/Fax: 01444 412202

Typeset and printed by
smallprint
35 Silver Birches
Haywards Heath
West Sussex RH16 3PD
01444 457101

Foreword by the Author

Teresa Giuccioli, the lady of Byron's love in Italy, wrote, some years after his death:

> Abroad, and above all in France, most biographies and estimates of Byron's character, through a union of superficiality and want of research, are based on hostile English books.

A few years ago a young Chinese woman who was doing postgraduate studies in Cambridge, asked the author, 'Why do the English hate Byron?' She told me that Byron is still an inspiration to Chinese students.

Soon after this young dissidents in Tiananmen Square were seen reading aloud from Byron's poetry.

Picture courtesy of
City of Nottingham Museums: Newstead Abbey

5

Contents

Byron's Reputation

I have now been compared to Nero, Apicius, Heliogabalus, Epicurus, Caligula, Henry VIII and the Devil. Were I to be beaten down by the world and its inheritors I would have succumbed long ago.

Byron, 1816

A year after his downfall and exile Byron wrote, 'England! with all thy faults I love thee still!' In 1817 he sent, 'A sigh to those who love me and a smile to those who hate.' In 1817 there were far more candidates for the smile than for the sigh and unhappily this is still true of Byron's countrymen today.

He had been treated atrociously by them from the beginning.

'No man ever lived who had such devoted friends,' Hobhouse had written, but equally no man ever lived who excited so strong a hatred in a large number of persons who had never set eyes on him.

Certainly he had given great offence morally, politically and poetically but this was not the entire cause of the animus. As a youth of nineteen at the innocuous outset of his career Byron had been selected by a serious journal as the victim of a review ferocious even by the standards then admissible and all through his literary life rages had broken out against him which now seem quite disproportionate to the affronts received. The epithets applied to him were on the whole much more severe than those used against Napoleon, the nation's enemy, and after his death there was only a lull before hostilities were resumed.

Doris Langley Moore

In 1822 the Reverend John Styles described the poet as a denaturalised human being who, having drained the cup of

9

sin to its bitterest dregs, is resolved to show that he is no longer human even in his frailties but a cool unconcerned fiend.

In 1823 the *Courier* wrote of him,

> With a brain from heaven and a pen that can write as angels speak and yet riots in thoughts that fiends might envy ... how worthless a thing is genius when divorced from religion from morals and humanity.

This was echoed in 1833 by Wordsworth who wrote to a Miss Kinnaird, 'What a monster is a man of genius whose heart is perverted.'

Over the years Byron became inured not only to bitter hostility but also downright calumny from complete strangers as well as acquaintances, though never from his friends. At nineteen he complained of, 'some damned old Tabbies,' at Southwell who accused him of, 'seducing no less than fourteen Damsels – besides sundry Matrons and Widows ... (not a fact I assure you).'

At thirty five he wrote wearily from Italy,

> I have seen the Blackwood; but I still think it a pity to prosecute ... Yet I am sure few have been libelled as I have been. Time sets things to rights.'

In Byron's case Time took an unconscionable time in doing so.

The worst of the libels were constructed after the abrupt ending of Byron's marriage and the rumours deriving from that event. The chief cause of these rumours was the calculated public silence of Lady Byron on the cause of the separation.

Byron himself was never vouchsafed an explanation –

> On the charges to be preferred against me – I have twice been refused any information by your father and his advisers:– it is now a fortnight – which has been passed in suspense – in humiliation – in obloquy – exposed to the most black and blighting calumnies of every kind – without even the power of contradicting conjecture and vulgar assertion as to the accusations.

Lady Byron was well aware of the effect her silence would have. 'The silence of my friends has been most disadvantageous to Byron as worse than the true causes are supposed.'

In private Lady Byron was anything but silent and some of her accusations can only be described as hysterical. She suspected that the staid and upright John Cam Hobhouse, Byron's truest friend, was helping him to conceal some terrible crime, probably murder, committed by Byron during their travels together. She further claimed to have known for a long time that under the guise of friendship Hobhouse was secretly working for Byron's ruin.

At her best Lady Byron was subtler than this. In a letter of instruction to her mother who was travelling to London to consult a lawyer Annabella wrote, 'I cannot swear to having been put in danger of my life at any one time, but only to my general conviction of danger.'

It is easy to imagine what defending counsel would have done with this vague conviction. It was never tested in court. Comments of this sort, carefully dropped here and there, led to such reactions as that of the Duchess of Devonshire, mother of Augustus Foster, one of Annabella's rejected suitors:

> Lady Byron's fate is the most miserable I ever heard and he must be mad or a Caligula. Caro will have told you some of the stories. It is too shocking and her life seems to have been endangered whilst with him from his cruelty.

The Duchess was not in the least enamoured of the girl who had rejected her son, 'She seemed good amiable and sensible, but she is cold prudent and calculating.' Later she added, 'an icicle'. Lady Byron succeeded in winning over people who positively disliked her.

The scandal of Byron's affair with Lady Caroline Lamb (the 'Caro' of the quotation above) two years earlier had already shocked London and had given Byron a lurid reputation. Caroline had threatened him, 'You have told me how foreign women revenge. Now you will see how an Englishwoman can.' The result was the stories mentioned by the Duchess which Caroline told not only to Lady Byron but to all those in London who would listen to a woman generally believed to be half mad with jealousy.

Byron's half-sister, Augusta Leigh, wrote, 'There are reports abroad too horrible to repeat.' Byron was in such anguish over the reports that she feared he would poison himself with laudanum. 'My name,' he wrote, 'has been as completely blasted as if it had been branded on my forehead.'

Among the rumours spread by Caroline Lamb was the accusation of homosexuality in an age of strong homophobia of which Louis Crompton gives a horrifying account in his book on *Byron and Greek Love*. The penalty for a homosexual act was death and the author gives a chilling account of the many who suffered the death penalty. Caroline Lamb's accusation was a serious matter and contributed to the general horror and hatred of Byron.

The consensus among scholars seems to be that Byron did not indulge in homosexual practices in England but may have done so towards the end of his first sojourn in Greece when he spent some time at a monastery outside Athens with a group of young boys. He was twenty three.

Louis Crompton treats Byron's interest in Greek love as his dominant sexual preoccupation. Impartial examination of the evidence shows it to have been an important but not a dominant factor. Mrs Langley Moore describes him not as homosexual but as sexually ambivalent.

Professor Leslie Marchand deals with Byron's attraction to younger boys at Harrow:

> Rejected by the girl he loved most desperately, he turned to the reassuring affection of his Harrow friends ... And so Byron developed a penchant for the society of younger boys ...

> If Byron had not clearly understood or admitted to himself the sexual implications of these passionate friendships at Harrow, he probably recognized this tendency in

himself while at Cambridge and certainly while he was in Greece on his first pilgrimage. There seems little doubt, if one considers the total evidence available, that a strong attraction to boys persisted in Byron from his Harrow days throughout his life ... But it seems just as evident that he felt no guilt or shame about any of the friendships he formed at Harrow.

Doris Langley Moore accepts Professor Marchand's account but questions the expression 'throughout his life'. 'There were substantial periods when, except in the ordinary course of friendship, he was not interested in any male.'

Professor Marchand agrees that 'Byron's attraction to women nevertheless did, on the whole, fulfil his needs much more extensively throughout longer periods of his life, though it was not necessarily stronger in individual instances.'

In an appendix to *Lord Byron: Accounts Rendered* Mrs Langley Moore gives a commonsense account of the matter:

> Byron was, in my belief, like many men of extreme sensibility, born with a genuinely bisexual temperament ... The stereotype of homosexual characteristics is no longer acceptable ... but there remain some indications which would still seem to be valid and most of them were notably absent in Byron ... he lacked masculine reserve and there was a tang of humorous malice in his gossip ... as a companion he had, when in a good mood, a cosiness ... that could make every occasion memorably intimate ... On the other hand he could be formidable in an essentially virile way and as for his style in literature – what could be less epicene?

There is no evidence that Byron was ever tempted to play anything but the active role in any sexual encounter. He and his Cambridge friends indulged in coded communication about a common interest in Greek love but there is not the slightest evidence that they were ever sexually interested in each other. At the end of his account of Byron's sexual ambivalence Professor Marchand writes:

These facts have long been known. Looked at without moral hysteria they help to explain a great deal in Byron's character and his relations with both men and women.

The contemporary hysteria against Lord Byron's moral offences was not much more ferocious than the furore caused by his political offences. In 1814 the *Lines to a Lady Weeping* were published over Byron's name. They were critical of the Prince Regent. Byron wrote to Lady Melbourne,

> The *Morning Post*, the *Sun*, *Herald*, *Courier*, have been in hysterics ever since – Did you ever know anything like this? At a time when peace and war Emperors and Napoleons – and the destinies of the things they have made of mankind are trembling in the balance – the Government Gazettes can devote half their attention and columns day after day to eight lines published two years ago and now republished only ... I begin to think myself really a most important person. What would poor Pope not have given to bring this down on his *Epistle to Augustus*?

This furore was as nothing to the consternation over his 1815 poems which purported to be translations from the French. These poems were regarded as pro-French, which indeed they were, and Byron was called a traitor. His recklessness in publishing these poems during the crisis of his separation from Lady Byron dismayed his friends but Byron refused to be silenced by self interest when he had something of burning importance to say. He was not concerned exclusively with the rights of Englishmen but with the Rights of Man. Arthur Symons wrote of him, 'Byron's thought embraced Europe as another man's thought might have embraced the village from which he had risen.'

Byron has been seen as the first international man, and people of many nations whose revolutions have been inspired by his poetry regard him as their countryman.

Even worse than the political offence of his poems was the reckless choice of subject of the poems published after his downfall and exile. *Don Juan* was regarded as depraved though Byron himself claimed that it was the most moral of poems. *The Examiner* defended him,

'You cavil at the jokes and irony of *Don Juan* as if you had found them in a sermon. But what right have you to comment on a satirical poem as if the author intended a sermon on the whole destiny of man?'

In fact the author did intend a sermon on the whole destiny of man, but it did not sound at all like a sermon and its satire was addressed to the author as well as to his audience. Byron never set up as a moral being on a higher plane than ordinary mortals. He left that sort of sermonizing to other Romantic poets.

The European Romantic Movement adopted Byron as the image of the Satanic anti-hero based on the sinister anti-heroes of his early poetry: *Childe Harold*, the *Giaour*, *Lara*, the *Corsair*. His influence was vast but it was based on the false belief that Byron was himself a Satanic figure. He contributed to this misunderstanding by his extraordinary frankness in talking about his failings and misdemeanours and by a disastrous tendency to exaggerate his peccadilloes. He delighted in shocking the censorious and the self-satisfied. When Byron described the exotic crimes of the heroes of the *Oriental Tales* his contemporaries imputed all these crimes to the author. He protested about this, in vain pointing out that other authors were never saddled with the crimes of their fictitious villains.

Once the image of the evil Satanic Byron had been created it became entrenched belief. His fame was extraordinary. Everything he did or said was reported or misreported not only throughout Europe and to the furthest boundaries of Russia, but also as far as America and South America. An American came to London expecting, so Byron said, to meet 'a misanthropist in wolf-skin breeches', and was rather disappointed to meet a sensible and gentlemanly poet who was a pleasant and amusing companion.

When Byron was a youth at Cambridge he invited his friends to Newstead Abbey and they used to fool about dressed up as monks drinking wine from a skull found in the grounds and romping with the parlour maids. This typical undergraduate behaviour was misreported years later by the French *Biographies of Famous Men* which solemnly informed its readers that Byron had murdered one of his mistresses and habitually drank wine out of her skull. Nanny Smith, the housekeeper at Newstead, later told Washington Irving that Byron and his friends had 'played some mad pranks but nothing but what young gentlemen do and no harm done'.

Pietro Gamba, the brother of the lady of Byron's love in Italy, Countess Giuccioli, warned his sister to have nothing to do with Byron because he had shut up his wife for several years in one of his castles for revenge. Pietro soon learned the truth and Byron was affectionately accepted into the Gamba family and entered into their plans for an uprising against the Austrian regime. Pietro accompanied Byron to Greece and wrote movingly of his death.

The attitude to Byron engendered by these rumours and canards is perpetuated by critics, reviewers and biographers who fail to take account of crucial research conducted over recent decades and in particular of *The Late Lord Byron* by Doris Langley Moore. No one who is familiar with the meticulous research by Mrs Moore into the motives and credentials of those who rushed into lucrative print after Byron's death could possibly rely on such sources as Medwin, Leigh Hunt, Trelawny or Lady Blessington.

Byron's Poetry

Yard after yard of rambling doggerel which occasionally crystallises into neat epigrams or even real poetry. Byron stands high among those writers in English ranging from Samuel Johnson to Virginia Woolf whose lives, letters journals and recorded talk are much more rewarding than the works which made them famous in the first place.

J W Lambert, *The Sunday Times,* 1982

… Why the fascination with Byron should have outlasted interest in his poetry.

Kathryn Hughes, *Daily Telegraph,* 1997

Byron was a most extraordinary and original writer – a genius of such power, complexity and versatility that he often confused the critics. He could do almost anything with poetry and did it, sometimes tongue-in-cheek. He is thought of as the quintessential Romantic, but he was also a product of the eighteenth century Enlightenment, an Augustan, a classicist, a realist and rationalist, whose purpose in his poetry was to set down on paper not what he wanted to see but what he saw.

For Byron truth as he saw it came before everything; though, as he saw it, truth was many-sided, complex, changing and even puzzling. So was his poetry. He cared nothing for politeness or decorum or saving faces, even his own. That would be cant or hypocrisy. He made no effort to tidy up reality. He described what he saw and then, if necessary, fought to change it. He never pretended that all was well when he knew that it was not. This annoyed many people in his own day and it is still annoying others today.

Why are the English so hostile to Byron? Why is his poetry underrated in England? These are questions often put to British Byronists – deeply embarrassing questions.

What Sir Arthur Quiller Couch wrote in 1922 is still true today: 'In these days a claim for Byron really needs pressing among his countrymen.' He added that this was 'an obstinate neglect born not of idleness or indifference but of positive reluctance to allow the claim'. He went on, 'This reluctance begins and ends at home. On the continent of Europe, through which his poetry first ran as a flame, it has endured and burned constantly.' He then protests, 'Byron belongs to us.'

The patronising attitude to Byron of many English critics today is fortunately not quite as complacent and insular as that of the perpetrator of the introduction to a selection of the poetry published by William Collins in 1941. The final paragraph concludes,

> The reason for his extraordinary popularity as a poet on the continent of Europe remains something of a mystery to the English reader. Romantic rhetoric was the fashion of the age, yet the greatest poets, such as Wordsworth and Shelley, escaped it. Their romantic outpourings were almost always controlled by thought. The frequent insincerity of Byron's sentiments combined with the inferior poetic technique of his lyrics harmed him in his native land. In his dramatic poems such as *Childe Harold* or *Manfred* the magnificent power of his oratory obscures the fact that his thought remains commonplace.

Presumably those ignorant foreigners across the Channel were hoodwinked by Byron's oratory into believing that what the English knew to be commonplace and insincere ranks among the greatest poetry ever written.

Those English who still share the attitude of the writer of that introduction should know that Byron's poetry still runs like a flame, not only through Europe but through the width of the world. It was put up on placards by *Solidarity* on the gates of the shipyard at Gdansk and carved on the three-crosses monument to those who died there. It was read aloud during the uprising in Tiananmen Square.

Outside England it goes without saying that those interested in the arts, in history, in politics, in epic poetry, in philosophy, read Byron. In England he is largely neglected and despised. Throughout the world he is known as a towering revolutionary figure and champion of the oppressed. In England he is most generally known as the seducer of Caroline Lamb. Even distinguished literary critics seem to be unaware of the enormous amount of work on Byron's life and poetry that is going on in universities all over the world.

The great twelve-volume edition of the letters and journals published by John Murray (descendant of Byron's original publisher) is the work of an American, Professor Leslie Marchand, who also produced in 1957 the great three-volume biography. The fine new edition of the poetry put out by Clarendon Press was edited by another American, Professor Jerome J McGann. There are branches of the Byron Society in Albania, Armenia, Australia, Austria, Belgium, Bulgaria, Canada, the Czech Republic, Cyprus, Denmark, Finland, France, Georgia, Germany, Greece, Holland, Hungary, Ireland, India, Lebanon, Malta, Mexico, New Zealand, Poland, Portugal, Romania, Russia, Spain, Sweden, Switzerland, Uruguay, the United States of America. Once a year the International Byron Society holds an academic conference. The *Byron Journal*, 'an invaluable collection of modern Byronic studies', comes out annually in London.

In Byron's own day his fame was world-wide. Augustine Burrell wrote, 'It is only by reading the lives and letters of his astonished contemporaries and immediate successors that you are able to form some estimate of the powers of Byron.' It is true that Goethe wrote, 'Byron alone I admit to a place at my side'; Barrès, 'Byron, le plus grand poète, et le plus grand philosophe. Son *Don Juan* est la plus haute philosophie'; that Lamartine called him, 'La plus grande nature poètique des temps modernes ... Je deviens ivre de sa poèsie'; and Shelley wrote of the first cantos of *Don Juan*, 'It is astonishingly fine – it sets him not above, but far above, all the poets of the day; every word has the stamp of immortality.'

These are fine tributes, but it is no longer necessary to look to Byron's contemporaries for a just appreciation of his genius. The late G Wilson Knight wrote,

> Byron is the only great poet since Shakespeare to possess one of Shakespeare's greatest gifts – that of pure artistic joy in the annals of human action in close association moreover with places. He feels the tingling nearness of heroic places.

He points out Byron's ability to love, 'not mankind, as Shelley, but men – and men and women of various sorts, places and times.'

He goes even further [and though a tendency to hyperbole is one of the chief joys of the writings of G Wilson Knight his judgement is nevertheless acute] –

> Indeed he was no ordinary man. He was a man of some new order as yet unrecognized. His descent may be traced to Greek tragedy, especially the *Prometheus Bound* and to what, in the *Golden Labyrinth* I called Shakespeare's dramatic supermen, and to all those who have tried to inject literary genius into the world of politics such as Dante, Milton and Swift.

The late Michael Cooke of Yale University wrote,

> His repeated demands for a poetry of truth, a poetry that was profitable to society, logical and moral, seems typically to have made over the terms he undoubtedly borrowed from the Enlightenment. Truth for him carries little of the idea of tradition and authority. It means candour and resolution in facing the voluminous problems of knowledge and experience.

Professor Cooke wrote of,

> His refusal of seductive substitutes for truth.

> Not just a particular standard of judgement but the very operation of judgement is called into question.

> Byron appears close to anticipating the orientation of modern linguistic philosophy.

Apparent confusion in his work results from an extraordinary accuracy in rendering the simultaneity of plural states. Critics have taken this as a random occurrence when it is a keynote of Byron's style.

Byron's own language is less categorical than paradoxical, approximating, revising and amplifying.

A man who has his principles and perceptions but without a temptation to canonise them as assertions and pronouncements.

Professor Andrew Rutherford wrote of *The Vision of Judgment* that it was,

Byron's masterpiece, aesthetically perfect, intellectually consistent, and morally profound.

Bernard Beatty of the University of Liverpool writes,

The thought in process in Byron's last poems – *The Island, The Deformed Transformed, Heaven and Earth* and the last cantos of *Don Juan*, is so ambitious in its scope, so exploratory, relentlessly paradoxical, yet so openly reactivating the inherited modes of European thought and value ...

The superiority of moral over aesthetic concerns was obvious to Byron.

In Byron we are always interested in the final verdict and unlike Coleridge Byron never avoids it.

Byron is in touch with more aspects of experience than his readers or critics are likely to be.

Anne Barton of the University of Cambridge wrote,

Don Juan is very much the work of retrospect. The work of an extraordinary lonely man looking back not only upon his own vanished life but upon that of an era. It is in a way, Byron's *A La Recherche du Temps Perdu*.

A preference for forms which echo the diffuse and sprawling patterns of human existence.

Don Juan like life, excluded nothing. It insists simultaneously upon conflicting points of view.

Michael Foot advises:

The best way to read *Don Juan* is to read it, not stopping, from beginning to end, all seventeen cantos. Only thus can the full force of the poem, the mixture of tragic and comic genius, be appreciated ... this is the surest way to measure its real greatness. Only thus can it be seen as Professor McGann described it, 'a conscious attempt to explain critically the meaning of the entire period in Europe stretching from 1789 to 1823'. Here was the epic which Shelley had urged him to write, the culminating achievement which made him the poet of the Revolution.

Although reading the critics is no substitute for reading Byron these few judgments show that there is no mystery about the high reputation of his poetry in Europe. The only mystery is his rejection by the English – excluding, of course, the academics, who, since they began in the nineteen sixties to read more carefully and with an open mind, know what they are talking about.

Byron's Politics

Lord Byron has gone to purchase admiration from the Greeks

An Italian spy, 1823

The man who had almost criminally evaded responsibility all his life, as Phyllis Grosskurth demonstrates, was suddenly meant to become the saviour of Greece

Peter Ackroyd, *The Times*, 1997

The astonishing claim made by Phyllis Grosskurth in her recent biography that Byron had spent a lifetime evading responsibility before he went to Greece does not survive the briefest scrutiny of his life. He fought to protect younger boys at Harrow and offered to take a beating for a weaker boy. He cared for and dosed his servants and they stayed with him all his life and accompanied him to Greece. He provided lavishly for his animals (as shown by Doris Langley Moore's analysis of his accounts), offered at fifteen to be the protector of his half-sister and helped her with money throughout his life, constantly gave to beggars, impoverished friends, funds for the Irish peasantry, hangers-on like Leigh Hunt, and the widows of his acquaintances. He spoke in Parliament in favour of Catholic Emancipation and Parliamentary reform long before these became acceptable causes. He put himself at risk in Italy by helping the Carbonari.

Much more important, both the writer and the reviewer who made and elaborated on this accusation seem to have failed to notice the awesome responsibility of producing, often for an inimical public, a vast body of poetry about the world and mankind and the whole terrifying and inescapable *lacrimae rerum*, laughing when he could, so that he might not weep. That laughter contributed largely to his undoing with the bigots of his own day and seems to have helped to blind his compatriots ever since to the virtues of his character and his poetry.

Byron was described by Professor Philip Collins as the only serious activist among the English Romantics and the only one with a European reputation. This gave Byron's words and actions compelling political influence. Even working men in England read his poetry avidly and believed that he would return and lead a revolution at the time of Peterloo. In Russia the Decembrist, Ryleyev, went to his execution with a copy of Byron's poems under his arm.

The image of Byron as champion of the oppressed is based not only on his activities in Italy and Greece but on the development of his thought which can be traced through his letters and journals and in his poetry from *Childe Harold* to the last cantos of *Don Juan*.

Byron came home from his unconventional Grand Tour with a powerful political poem. In *Childe Harold* cantos one and two Byron attacked the ruling classes in Spain for their cowardice in the face of the enemy, and praised the common people of Spain for their courage and resistance. He mocked the perpetrators of the Convention of Cintra, and accused Lord Elgin, a distinguished peer and former Ambassador to the Porte, of robbing Greek temples. He described the horrors of war and, even more annoying for the powers that be, the stupidity of those who engaged in it. He called on the Greek people to rise against the Turks and win their freedom.

He made it clear in later years what he meant by freedom; neither monarch, foreign conqueror, oligarchy or mob must ever be allowed to tyrannize over the people. He warned that he would always take the side of the weak against the tyrant even if that tyrant happened in a particular case to be the mob. For this many of the Left are unable to forgive him.

Yet one cannot doubt his sympathy with the people. In his maiden speech he told the House of Lords,

> You call these men a mob. Are you aware of your obligations to a mob? It is the mob that labour in your fields and serve in your houses, that man your navy and recruit your army, that have enabled you to defy the world

24

and can also defy you when neglect and calamity have driven them to despair.

Years later in Greece Byron, as reported by William Parry who was with him over the last months in Missolonghi, spoke of the Greek peasantry,

> No system of government in any part of Greece can be permanent which does not leave in the hands of the peasantry the chief part of the political power. They are warmly attached to their country and they are the best portion of the people. Under a government in the least degree equitable they must increase rapidly both in numbers and wealth; and unless they are placed, in a political point of view, on an equality with other classes it will soon be necessary to oppress them.

John Mortimer has pointed out that the poetry of this young aristocrat was always at the service of the common people. This made Byron suspect to the government of the day. Even more suspect was the fact that he cared nothing for the necessities of the government's foreign policy. When everyone in England was rejoicing at the defeat of Napoleon Byron was horrified at the restoration of the Bourbons which put an end to the hopes engendered by the French revolution.

> How [wrote the Reverend Sydney Smith] can any man stop in the stupendous joy of getting rid of Napoleon after all these years of war and prophesy the little piddling evils that will result from the restoration of the Bourbons?

Though this was a natural and understandable reaction he went further, admitting that he rather wanted Paris burned both for security and revenge. Byron's attitude was distinctly more magnanimous.

When he was living in Italy Byron helped the Carbonari to try to win their freedom from the Austrian regime. He travelled dangerously to Greece to help the Greeks win their independence from Turkey. He went at the request of the Greek Committee in London who knew that his support would

25

be of incalculable value in drumming up support for the Greeks and in raising a Greek loan.

It is typical of Byron's fate that his motives were immediately impugned although this was the culmination of a lifetime's preoccupation with the problem of tyranny. An Italian spy wrote, 'Lord Byron is gone to purchase adoration from the Greeks.' He did take large sums of money with him for buying medical supplies, building fortifications and paying troops but he was far too experienced to expect adoration in return. When their revolt collapsed the Italians had quietly returned the weapons he had got for them to his cellars thus putting him in danger from the Austrians. His only comment was, 'It is no great matter who or what is sacrificed supposing Italy could be liberated. It is a great object. The very poetry of politics.'

The following comments could be applied to Bosnia today. Byron would have made a fine Secretary General of UNO.

A military man who knew Byron in Greece wrote, 'He spoke with vehemence and indignation of the conduct of Europe and her apathy and neglect of the greatest of causes.' He also gave Byron credit for having wakened the Greeks to a desire for freedom.

Byron's attitude to the Greek campaign as reported by William Parry is admirable in its lack of hubris and its down to earth common sense.

I am here to act against the external enemies of Greece and tyrants of Greece and will not take part with any faction in the country. We who come here to fight for Greece have no right to meddle with its internal affairs or dictate to the people or government.

He also made it clear,

I have no enmity to the Turks individually. They are quite as good as the Greeks. I am displeased to hear them called barbarians. They are charitable to the poor and very humane to animals.

Byron understood the complexity of the situation in Greece and recognized the delicacy of the choices before him.

> We must not suppose under our name of Greeks an entire united and single people kept apart from all others by strongly marked geographical or moral distinctions. On the contrary. Those who are now contending for freedom are a mixed race of various tribes of men having different apparent interests and different opinions. Many of them differ from and hate each other more even than they differ from and hate the Turks.

Byron has been criticised for refusing to throw in his lot with one or other of the Greek factions and compared unfavourably with Trelawny (especially by Trelawny) who rushed off to join the robber chieftain, Odysseus, whose chief object was to get his hands on Byron's money and who very shortly went over to the Turks. If Byron had followed his example he would have damaged the cause irrevocably and earned the contempt of the international community.

In *Don Juan* Byron shows that he is aware of the great danger of all revolutions – that the revolutionaries may themselves become tyrants. No one may be allowed to tyrannize over the people. Even the poet will not seek to impose his will on them – 'I wish men to be free/As much from mobs as kings, from you as me.' Unfortunately Byron's courage and common sense have never been appreciated by his countrymen. He would have been philosophical about it. He warns of what happens to those who get involved in politics to help their fellow men:

> When a man hath no freedom to fight for at home
> Let him combat for that of his neighbours,
> Let him think of the glories of Greece and of Rome
> And get knocked on the head for his labours.

> To do good to mankind is the chivalrous plan
> And is always as nobly requited.
> Then battle for freedom wherever you can
> And if not shot or hanged you'll get knighted.

Byron certainly didn't 'get knighted'. The Greeks wanted to bury him in their Temple of Theseus. Westminster Abbey turned away not only his body but also his statue, which now stands in the library of Trinity College Cambridge.

In the year of the Bicentenary of Byron's birth, 1988, the Russians struck a commemorative stamp with Byron's head on it. Newstead Abbey asked for a British stamp to commemorate the Bicentenary and it was refused. One of those who got a commemorative stamp that year was Edward Lear, a very fine though minor painter and a writer of superlative nonsense rhymes. I wonder whether there is a moral in that.

Byron's Women

All the chilly degrees of his cold heartedness …

… his neglected daughter, Allegra

Peter Ackroyd, *The Times*

I cannot exist without some object of love   Byron

Byron was a Regency nobleman and Regency noblemen were not renowned for their chastity. Byron did not claim to be any better than his peers and in fact made himself out to be much worse than he was. He went in for dissolute behaviour at certain clearly defined periods of his life but he did not treat women as objects and he was considerate even of the women of the town.

As a young man Byron was afraid that his deformity, the lameness about which he was morbidly sensitive, would make it impossible, 'for such a one as I am ever to be beloved.' He had heard his early love, Mary Chaworth tell her maid that she could, 'never love that lame boy.' He needed to prove his power over women both to himself and to his friends. When at the age of nineteen he spent some weeks in London he boasted to his friends of such sexual feats with his blue-eyed Caroline that a doctor had prescribed bed rest for both of them, presumably in beds far removed from each other. When his Caroline [mistakenly] feared that she was pregnant he told his friends much to their consternation that he must marry her.

Another period of wildly dissolute behaviour followed the break-up of his marriage, his rejection by London society and his voluntary exile. In Venice he boasted of two hundred sexual encounters, which Du Bos claimed was a natural reaction to the strait-laced conduct of his wife. Byron did claim that,

> What Gods call gallantry and men adultery
> Is much more common where the climate's sultry.

But this was a period when he was pouring out energy in an incredible output of brilliant plays and poems. One partner, his blue-eyed Caroline, had exhausted him at the age of 19. Perhaps his stamina was much improved by 27, but it seems to me more likely that he was exaggerating wildly to show his priggish wife to what lengths she had driven him.

Apart from such periods of promiscuity Byron tended to love one woman at a time and he behaved honourably and on the whole kindly to the women in his life. He was not kind to Lady Byron, and his relations with her will be dealt with in another chapter. It is relevant here, however, to consider the remark made by Byron's valet, Fletcher: 'Every lady could manage my Lord except my Lady.'

As a young man Byron behaved rebelliously to his mother and he quite failed to recognize and appreciate the sacrifices she made for him. He was dismayed by her violent rages, sometimes referred to her as 'Mrs Byron Furiosa' and told how she once threw the fire irons at him and laid him flat. His half-sister, Augusta Leigh, said that the scenes Mrs Byron made with her young son 'were enough to spoil the very best disposition and temper'. But later, when a journalist attacked his mother, Byron leaped to her defence: 'My mother has foibles enough but not a single vice.'

When Byron became famous he was pursued by women. Even his early love, Mary Chaworth, tried to reawaken his interest in her. In almost every case he was not the hunter but the hunted.

Byron has been portrayed as the heartless seducer of Lady Caroline Lamb. Here is the true story: Having read the first two cantos of *Childe Harold*, which were the talk of London, Lady Caroline, married and with a small son (whose development was tragically retarded through epilepsy), declared, 'I must meet this new poet if he is ugly as Aesop.' He was not. She was determined that he should love her and he was briefly beguiled into falling madly in love. But very soon Byron saw that her behaviour was so wildly indiscreet that he must either run away with her or end the affair. He withdrew. She pursued him relentlessly and when packed off to Ireland by her anxious family wrote frenzied letters to Byron boasting of her conquests there. Byron wrote to Lady Melbourne, who had become his confidante, 'I cannot write. I would not seem jealous but it would be improper to appear indifferent.'

He admitted generously, 'She never did nor can deserve a single reproach which must not fall with double justice and truth on me.' He wanted to be free of her,

If I can honourably be off – Manage her? It is impossible! and as to friendship – no – it must be broken off at once and all I have left is to take some step to make her hate me.

If she throws herself upon me *"cosi finiva"*, if not, the sooner it is over the better.

I am much more unwilling now to hurt her feelings than ever. She has a claim on me for every respect that she may not feel her own degradation.

She tells me she could make anyone in love with her.

I am sick of scenes and want quiet.

Good God, am I to be hunted from place to place like a Russian bear?

Is she mad or mischievous only?

What she says of me I can guess from what she says of others.

Mr Lamb found Caroline in tears. Wroth to a degree and wanted to hear if I (the most inoffensive of men) had offended her – if I speak to her he is insulted – if I don't speak to her she is insulted.

Byron felt that if Caroline did in fact run away from her husband he was in honour bound to marry her:

If after all, I must be hers she shall be mine as long as it pleases her. Wretched as it would render me she should never know it.

31

Caroline never did run away from her husband so Byron was not called upon to make the sacrifice.

Byron now offered marriage to Annabella Milbanke (Lady Melbourne's niece from the north country whom he had met at Melbourne House). She had interested him for some time. Annabella turned him down. Byron took refuge with an older woman, Lady Oxford, who encouraged him in his political career. Lord Oxford was a conniving husband. Their tribe of engaging children all bore the name of Harley but some were said to resemble sundry former lovers of Lady Oxford and they were known as the Harleian Miscellany. After a while Lord Oxford began to cut up rough and seems to have threatened to throw his wife out of the house. Although she was well over forty and he only twenty four, Byron immediately offered her a *carte blanche*, upon which (to Byron's intense relief), Lord Oxford, 'ate up his words and his intentions and they are to live happy ever after.'

From the moment when Byron met his half-sister, Augusta, at the age of fifteen, he took her to his heart and offered to be her protector though she was by five years the elder. This shows the generosity of his disposition for he might have envied her upbringing in the aristocratic circles from which he had been excluded. He spent most of his childhood in an apartment in Aberdeen and a modest house in Nottingham. Although Lord Carlisle was his guardian he was never invited to stay at the grand house in Grosvenor Square or at Castle Howard where Augusta was treated as one of the family.

After the break with Lady Oxford Byron squired Augusta (now married to Colonel Leigh) about town and was soon passionately in love with her. Lady Melbourne was horrified at this dangerous liaison and persuaded Byron to visit his friend Wedderburn Webster who had a pretty wife, Lady Frances. She hoped Lady Frances would lure him away from his half-sister. Byron wrote from Aston,

Lady Frances evidently expects to be attacked and seems prepared for a brilliant defence. My character as *rouè* has gone before me and my careless and quiet behaviour astonished her. She began to think herself ugly or me blind.

He joked about the situation, but he was falling in love again. He told Lady Melbourne, 'Platonism was in some peril. Her husband runs after every little country girl and boasts of it. He must not be surprised if others admire that which he knows not how to value.' Byron said he would have looked after her better. 'She is so thin and pale. If she were once my wife a warm climate would be the first resort for her recovery.'

He was amused by Lady Frances's religious airs, but when she offered herself to him but told him she knew she would regret it, he 'spared her'. 'It was not the "no" one has heard so often before. She meant it.' This seems to me doubtful. She kept on sending him cryptic messages and he told Lady Melbourne, 'If people will stop at the first tense of the verb *aimer* they must not be surprised if one finishes the conjugation with someone else.'

Byron half confided in Lady Melbourne his passion for Augusta and his wish to go abroad with her. Lady Melbourne told him this would mean utter social ruin for Augusta and for himself. Augusta and he decided that he must marry.

Annabella Milbanke had initiated a new correspondence with him by misrepresenting herself as hopelessly in love with another so that Byron would not take fright at the possibility of an entanglement. Almost on the toss of a coin he asked her whether her objections were insuperable and Annabella took this to be a proposal of marriage. She had captured her poet.

After the separation Byron was pursued by an eighteen-year-old girl, Claire Clairmont, whose step sister, Mary Godwin, had run away with the poet Shelley. Hoping to catch a more famous poet than her sister, she accosted Byron and persistently threw herself at his head. She suggested that they should travel about ten miles outside London and spend the night together. Byron disliked this sort of behaviour intensely, but in the end he succumbed and the result was

Allegra, whom Byron offered to bring up as long as the mother would leave him alone:

> I never loved or pretended to love her but a man is a man and if a girl comes prancing to you at all hours there is but one way.

From Switzerland he wrote,

> All these mistresses! I have had but one. Now don't scold, but what could I do? A foolish girl, in spite of all I could say or do, would come after me. I have had all the plagues possible to persuade her to go back again but at last she went. I could not exactly play the stoic with a woman who had scrambled 1000 miles to unphilosophise me.

In Venice Byron was pursued yet again, this time by a draper's wife of great beauty who ran away from her husband to live with him. He tried to persuade her to go back but,

> As the morals of this place are very lax, all the women say she has done right, especially her own relations. You needn't be alarmed. I know how to manage her. She is extremely fond of Allegra.

On one occasion this man reputed to be so harsh to women wrote, 'Marianna is not very well today and I shall stay with her and nurse her this evening.'

Marianna sold some jewels he had given her and was succeeded by Margarita Cogni, the baker's wife, the *Fornarina*. She was a passionate beauty who once threw herself into the Grand Canal in a jealous tantrum. Byron wrote of this episode,

> Thomas Moore told me that at Geneva they had made a devil of a story of the *Fornarina* – young lady seduced – subsequent abandonment – leap into the Grand Canal – her being in the madhouse as a consequence. I should like to know who was nearest being made mad and be damned to them.

This sort of 'devil of a story', similarly unfounded, was being told all over Europe.

It is hard to believe, but the young mother, Claire Clairmont, sent Allegra over to Byron in Italy at little more than twelve months old. Later he lent Claire a villa so she could spend some time with Allegra, but declined to see the mother for fear that the result would be an addition to the family.

After a time Byron asked his friends, the Hoppners, to look after Allegra for him. His household in Venice was not suitable for a small girl. After moving to Ravenna he sent for her. He went to great pains over Allegra, asking the Hoppners to investigate schools in Switzerland; but, after a time, finding she was beyond the control of the servants, he put her in a convent school in a country town where the air was better than that of Ravenna. Claire wrote insulting letters to him about his care of the child and he wrote to Hoppner,

> Were it not for the poor little child's sake I am tempted to send her back to her atheistical mother. But that would be too bad. She shall be a Christian and a married woman. I have been to great care and expense, taking a house in the country on purpose for her. She has two maids and every possible care and attention. The heat has been intense. Take care of your little boy.

He was determined that Allegra should not go to the Shelley household where Claire was now living.

> I so totally disapprove of the mode of children's treatment in their family. Have they reared one? The child shall not quit me again to perish of starvation or green fruit.

Allegra fell ill of a fever and died in the convent, much to the distress of the nuns who adored her. One of them retired to bed with a nervous breakdown as a result of the little girl's death.

This, too, was made into 'a devil of a story' about the wicked Lord Byron who cared nothing for his child and let her die in a strict convent where the nuns were cruel to her. It was said that Byron refused to go to her when he heard she was seriously ill, but Mrs Doris Langley Moore studied the postmarks and has proved that the letter announcing the child's death came before the letter warning that she was seriously ill.

Some have accused Byron of callousness towards Claire, but her pursuit of him was so tenacious that he dared not encourage her. He could not have lived with her for one week, let alone a lifetime. In the circumstances all he could do was to support the little girl and make sure she would be educated and later given sufficient dowry to achieve a reasonable marriage.

The tone of Claire Clairmont's mind can be judged from two entries in her *Journals*:

> The deformity of your mind surpasses all that can be imagined of monstrous, but in your birth Nature had set her warning mark on you, unheeding that by my own blindness have I fallen.

And, on the subject of her sister, Mary Shelley, who had suggested to her that Byron's intention of having the little girl educated in a superior convent with other children, some of rank, would be a sensible plan:

> Would to God she could perish without note or remembrance.

His last love was the young Italian countess, Teresa Giuccioli. Having made her his mistress at her own request he felt responsible for her happiness and for the reputation she gaily risked by calling out to him 'Mio Byron' at receptions in Venice. He wrote to Hobhouse,

> If she and her husband make it up you may see me in England. If not, I will retire to France or America with her, change my name and lead a quiet provincial life. All this may seem odd but I have got the girl into a scrape.

He assured Teresa that she would be his last passion, but Greece intervened. He felt responsible for her and this made it difficult for him to break away, but break away he did and set out from Genoa assuring her that they would meet again.

Byron's Marriage

The marriage of Lord Byron to Annabella Milbanke aroused avid speculation. Today they would figure regularly in the magazine called *Hello*. The *Morning Herald* considered it a union of 'two such interesting persons'. The Prince Regent cried, 'Between her Prose and his Poetry what may we not expect?' Annabella was an heiress and Byron discovered, 'She is a kind of pattern in the North.' She was reputed to be the most virtuous and high-minded of young women, a blue stocking, a mathematician, Byron's 'Princess of Parallelograms'. The idea of a young man with so wild a reputation being tied to such a strait-laced young woman intrigued the gossips. When Byron left England after the scandal of the separation John Murray, his publisher, offered Polidori, the doctor he had hired to accompany him on his travels, five hundred pounds for any diary he might keep on their journey, for a travel book.

When Annabella changed her mind about rejecting Byron and set in motion her plan for reeling him in, she still had grave doubts about his suitability as a husband. But she had allowed no less than five eligible suitors to slip through her fingers and the old friend, Hugh Montgomery, whom she kept on a string to guard against the possibility of being left an old maid, was not very impressive. The 'first poet of the age' would be a considerable catch.

Byron had to travel up to Seaham, a village on the bleak Northumbrian coast, where the Milbankes led a cosy, provincial existence full of private family jokes – teasing each other about food and visits to the lavatory, gossiping about their neighbours, taking part in local politics and parading their strict views on piety and religion. It was no fit milieu for a wayward genius. On one of his visits Byron wrote to Thomas Moore, 'I must go to tea. Damn tea! I wish it were Kinnaird's brandy.'

He had told Lady Melbourne, 'I mean to reform most

thoroughly and become "a good man and true". I will endeavour to make your niece happy.'

Annabella soon sent him away for fear they might anticipate the marriage.

His affairs were in a parlous state. He was determined to arrange a generous settlement for Annabella, but his agent, Hanson, was dilatory and the Milbankes were clamouring for him to return to meet Annabella's uncle, Lord Wentworth, who had a large fortune to leave.

Byron was not mercenary. He wrote, 'I don't know whether Annabella has any fortune but if nothing I'll sell Newstead again as I can then give her a better settlement.'

The lure of Lord Wentworth's wealth failed to get him up to Seaham in time for the meeting.

The sale of Newstead (which fell through) would have paid his debts and provided 'a surplus for necessities'.

He asked Annabella if, in view of this financial disaster, she would prefer to wait, but a positive chorus of reproach came from Seaham summoning him back before the wedding cake went mouldy. By the time he came they had to bake a new one.

The settlement finally negotiated between Byron's agent Hanson and Sir Ralph Milbanke settled £65,000 (depending on the future sale of Newstead Abbey) on Annabella and her children. Sir Ralph was in financial difficulties and could offer as dowry no more than six thousand pounds, which was never paid. Annabella had expectations but Byron made no stipulation regarding her fortune. Hanson told him the Milbankes were grasping.

Annabella had told Byron that secrecy about their engagement was no longer necessary, and without consulting him she told all her friends. Byron had to send off urgently to Lady Melbourne, 'Tell Caro!'

Both Annabella and Byron were beginning to suspect that they were not the most compatible couple. Each offered the other the opportunity to withdraw. Unfortunately for both they failed to do so. Byron wrote to Annabella,

I can conceive of no misery equal to mine if I fail to make you happy and yet how can I do justice to those merits from whose praise there is not a dissentient voice?

He wrote to Hobhouse,

I wish it was well over. I do hate bustle. They tell me I must not marry in a black coat and I can't bear a blue one. Forgive my nonsense. I must be serious for the rest of my life.

Hobhouse knew that Byron was a reluctant bridegroom. 'Never was lover less in haste.' When Annabella and Byron drove off on their honeymoon Hobhouse wrote, 'I felt as if I had buried a friend.'

Annabella's account of the honeymoon is well known. We have no account of it from Byron.

When the young couple returned to London they moved into a grand house on Piccadilly Terrace whose rent they could ill afford since the expected dowry was not forthcoming.

The rumour was that Byron had married an heiress, so his creditors descended on him in force. A few months later they returned when Lord Wentworth died unexpectedly. The duns were convinced that Lord Byron's wife had inherited, whereas in fact everything went to Lady Milbanke. The bailiffs moved in and Byron's books had to be sold. Lady Byron failed to understand Byron's horror and humiliation at these events. She had never been short of money and never would be. Byron had brought it all on himself by the profligate spending of his youth, but that made it no easier to bear.

Though there is no doubt that Byron was an impossible husband, Augusta (or any other woman, according to Fletcher), would have known how to manage him.

Hobhouse explained that Lady Byron was incapable of understanding Byron's foibles,

... founding her opinions upon sundry playful paradoxes of which a total inapprehension of irony and humour of any kind prevented her from appreciating the

39

true value. It is true that Lord Byron, upon discovering that his new companion did not understand him so entirely as his old friends, should have desisted from these extravagances of expression and manner which ... were set down to the account of a depraved mind rejoicing in the contemplation of every enormity.

Byron told Annabella that they would get on very well if she paid less attention to his words. He told Hobhouse that he got up late, was often out of spirits and sometimes out of humour. He was suffering from an illness which caused Augusta great anxiety. We hear of no concern over this illness from Lady Byron.

One important cause of friction must have been Byron's strange behaviour over food. Annabella had written from Seaham to tell him she had engaged a cook for them. Nothing could have made Byron more uneasy. He never dined regularly but starved himself most of the time, firstly to maintain the slim figure he had achieved by dieting and exercise after becoming exceedingly overweight as a boy, and secondly because he believed frugality over eating helped to control the passions (not merely sexual) and he did not care to be subject to passion.

He has been mocked for affectation because he dined on potatoes and vinegar at his first dinner with Samuel Rogers. Rogers told the story that Byron went straight out from his house to eat a hearty meal, and he claimed to have learned this from Hobhouse. Doris Langley Moore has established that Hobhouse was not in England at that time.

Byron's letters show that he used to starve himself for days and then eat like a lion. 'I have unfortunately dined for the week yesterday evening' – 'I have lived on tea and bread and butter since leaving Eywood.' And, to Samuel Rogers, 'May I come after dinner tonight as I have so bedevilled my digestion that your light supper the other night nearly killed me.'

Lady Byron had a hearty appetite and her letters to her

40

parents dwell lovingly on food. Byron once said frivolously that a woman should never be seen eating except lobster salad and champagne. 'I once begged a lady to refrain from eating more than one fowl at a sitting, to no effect.'

It must have been very upsetting for Annabella to find that conjugal dinners would be rare events and that Byron did not care for giving dinner parties which included women. She was used to the pleasant family table in her parents' house. She must have felt very lonely. She was very young and she soon became pregnant. The arrival of the motherly Augusta must have been a great relief until she began to harbour suspicions of her new sister's former relationship with Byron.

Byron was now drinking heavily. Otherwise he might have been more considerate. On the other hand Annabella was marrying a genius. A more perceptive and less inflexible woman, who loved him, would have tried to fit in with his ways instead of trying to change him. She even tried to discourage him from writing poetry and would walk into the room when he was writing. He told that she would gaze at him with a mixture of pity and anxiety.

He refused to meet her friends (who were unfortunately the sort who were sure to find Byron's conversation shocking, and who would have bored him to distraction). He told Hobhouse that he would come home and find his wife sitting with a crowd of Old Blues who thought a man damned if he made a joke.

Byron described the year of the marriage in one of his pleas to Lady Byron after they had parted.

The trial has not been very long. A year I grant you – of distress – and distemper – and misfortune but these fall chiefly on me – and bitter as the recollection is to me of what I have felt – it is much more so to have made you a partaker of my desolation.

A year after the wedding Lady Byron had taken her month-old daughter to visit her parents, at Byron's request, and left

Byron forever, refusing to give any reason for her demand for a separation. Byron's memoirs were burned soon after news of his death reached England so we are unlikely ever to see his own account of the marriage. All we have is the uncorroborated version of one of the parties to a broken marriage. Byron admitted to many faults, and we have the testimony of Augusta's letters that he was drinking heavily and that his behaviour became increasingly violent and bizarre; though there are no claims that he was physically violent to his wife, even from her. Byron pleaded illness and desperation over his debts and the presence of bailiffs in the house. He begged Annabella to return and promised to reform. She was implacable.

5th February 1816

Dearest Bell – No answer from you yet – perhaps it is as well – but do recollect – that all is at stake – the present – the future – and even the recollection of the past:– The whole of my errors or what harsher name you choose to call them – you know – but I loved you – and will not part from you without your own most express and *expressed* refusal to return to or receive me – only say the word – that you are still mine in your heart – and "Kate! – I will buckler thee against a million" – Ever yours dearest most   B

Lady Byron conceived the completely false idea that Byron would try to deprive her of custody of the little girl, Ada. She believed it her duty to blacken the names of both Byron and Augusta in order to prevent this.

On 12th February, 1816 Hobhouse learned from George Byron, a strong supporter of Lady Byron who was staying at Piccadilly Terrace, of

very great tyranny, menaces, furies, neglects and even real injuries such as telling his wife he was living with another woman and actually in fact turning her out of the house [when she left for Seaham with Ada]. I got him to own much of what I had been told in the morning. He was dreadfully agitated said he was ruined and would blow out his brains.

Byron prepared a statement soon after this:

Lady Byron may have had cause to complain of my temper. My manner may have been harsh and rude, perhaps occasionally insulting. My pecuniary distresses and my ill state of body, increased by no very infrequent excesses resorted to for the sake of oblivion, may have made me appear half frantic, but my violence was never directed towards my wife. I made no secret of my hating marriage, but was equally explicit in avowing my love for her. If she can prove that each day I said or did something to give her pain, I can prove that not a day passed without my appearing at least to afford her satisfaction. She may have seen me sullen, silent or morose but she has often been herself surprised sitting on my knee with her arm around my neck. If I was often neglectful I was more often fond. I may have been indiscreet – perhaps too much so. I poured out all my confessions into her ear, told her of all my failings, never committed a fault without making her my confidante. Even those errors which must have been most offensive to herself, whether in word or deed, were communicated with an unreserve which may have been mistaken for insult but which was not meant for such. The allegations at which she hints, my respect for her character and confidence in her veracity, almost make me think must have some foundation and I am therefore inclined at times to believe that at some periods of my married life I might have been deprived of reason for I solemnly protest that I am unconscious of the commission of any enormity which can have prompted Lady Byron to desert me thus suddenly, thus cruelly.

Hobhouse writes,

A horrid story of Lord Byron having asked his wife when in labour whether the child was dead, having become common, his friends put the question to him and his sister. He answered that he was content to rest the whole merits of his case upon Lady Byron's simple assertion in

43

that respect. 'She will not say so,' he frequently repeated, 'though, God knows, poor thing – it seems now she would say anything: but she would not say that.'

Of some of the rumours, Byron wrote to his wife that they 'imply a treatment I am incapable of inflicting or you of imputing.'

Lady Byron's imputations became more and more damning over the long years of self-justification. In 1818 she was already capable of writing,

> I clung to an hypothesis repeatedly overthrown – that there was some secret good at the bottom of his heart – though such motives were never evidenced and such delusion will always be liable to return.

The story of the marriage as told by Lady Byron was implicitly believed on the grounds that she was so high minded and truthful a woman that she was incapable of lying. Extracts from some of her letters at the time of the separation put the reputed high-mindedness in some doubt.

> I'm told he is threatening his friends with suicide. A *professed* intention of that sort is rather amusing.

> My mother says that if he does take laudanum so much the better. It is not fit such men should live.

> He is more jealous of his character than anyone in the world. Could we not use this to bring him to terms?

> Mrs Ellison says now one will have an opportunity of learning who are bad and good – that there never was a question which disclosed morals so clearly – except Lady Melbourne and Lady Bessborough pour moi – indeed I don't know anybody except the Piccadilly crew of blackguards who is avowedly against me.

She brought him to terms and hounded him out of the country. When a solitary newspaper defended Byron, her father visited the editor and tried to suppress any comment favourable to Byron.

Here are some of Lady Byron's comments on Byron's friends:

Of Augusta Leigh, who dearly loved Byron,

Mrs Leigh will do anything for Byron and for the worst motive – profit.

Of Mrs Musters,

Such a wicked looking cat. Someone else looks quite virtuous by her side. [Caroline Lamb]

Of Hobhouse, Byron's loving friend who defended him through thick and thin,

I have known for many months now that under the guise of friendship Hobhouse has been endeavouring Byron's ruin.

Of her aunt, Lady Melbourne,

I shall cut her. Do you think I ought? I don't know what good she can ever do me.

So much for Lady Byron.

Later Byron changed his mind about his wife's 'veracity':

... trust in thy truth,
And the wild fame of my ungoverned youth –
On things that were not and on things that are,
Even on such a basis hast thou built
A monument whose cement has been guilt,
The moral Clytemnestra of thy lord! ...

... But of thy virtues didst thou make a vice,
Trafficking with them for a purpose cold,
For present anger and for future gold –
And buying others grief at any price.
And thus once entered into crooked ways
The early truth which was thy proper praise
Did not still walk beside thee – but at times,
And with a breast unknowing its own crimes,
Deceit, averments incompatible,

Equivocations, and the thoughts which dwell
In Janus spirits – the significant eye
Which learns to lie with silence – the pretext
Of prudence, with advantages annexed –
The acquiescence in all things which tend,
No matter how, to the desired end –
All found a place in thy philosophy.

A piece published in Blackwoods in 1869 sets out the anomalies in Byron's condemnation by the righteous on the sole grounds of Lady Byron's secret testimony:

She lives with her husband for more than a year without communicating to her own parents or to anyone else any cause for discomfort. She leaves him without the slightest indication of displeasure. She tries to prove him mad; failing that, she declares her determination never to return to him. Through her mother she lays before Dr Lushington a statement of her case. He (no doubt very wisely) advises a reconciliation. Failing with Dr Lushington as she had with Dr Baillie, she seeks a personal interview, and then, in the secrecy of his Chambers under the seal of a confidence stricter than that of the confessional, she imparts to him something which he is bound to assume on her sole assurance to be true – which he was, without investigation or inquiry, to accept as the basis of his opinion – which he was, under no circumstances whatever, without her express authority (an authority which death has now put it out of her power to give) to divulge, upon which she obtains his opinion that a reconciliation was impossible. What that something was we shall probably never know but, save in the case of the victims who were sent to the guillotine on suspicion of being suspected, we know of no condemnation so monstrous, so revolting to every principle of justice and common sense as that which has been passed on Lord Byron.

Some years later Byron commented sadly on the loss of his daughter. In July 1821 he received a letter from a dying girl in England,

46

... who could not go out of the world without thanking me for the delight which my poesy for several years etc. She begged me to burn her letter which I cannot do as I look upon such a letter in such circumstances as better than a diploma from Gottingen. I had a similar tribute from Norway in 1819. These are the things which make one at times believe oneself a poet. What a strange thing is life and man. If I were to present myself at the door of the house where my daughter now is the door would be shut in my face but if I had gone to Droitheim, the furthest town in Norway, I would have been received with open arms into the mansion of strangers and foreigners.

Byron's Friendships

He was treacherous towards all his friends

Christopher Hudson, *Daily Mail*, 1997

It is not easy to write about someone whose behaviour was consistently cruel, careless and self serving

Kathryn Hughes, *Daily Telegraph*, 1997

Difficult as a lover, impossible as a husband, Byron was loyal and generous as a friend, lavish to a fault in his appreciation. It was hard on him that any unguardedly facetious or impatient utterance he made was liable to be turned into a weapon of attack by contending parties.

Doris Langley Moore, 1961

William Harkness, who had known him at Harrow, wrote after his death,

I have many slights and neglects towards him to reproach myself with but I cannot call to mind a single instance of caprice or unkindness in the whole course of our friendship to allege against him.

John Pigot knew him well at Southwell from the age of fifteen to twenty –

Few people understood Byron but I knew that he had naturally a kind and feeling heart and that there was not a single spark of malice in his composition.

Francis Hodgson wrote,

Were it possible to state all he has done for numerous friends he would appear amiable indeed. For myself I am bound to acknowledge in full and warmest manner his most generous and well-timed aid, and were my poor friend Bland alive he would gladly bear the same testimony.

Lady Holland wrote after Byron's death,

[Lady Byron] could not fail to have loved Byron. He was such a lovable person. I remember him sitting there with the light upon him, looking so beautiful.

Hobhouse wrote, 'No man ever lived who had such devoted friends'. Their letters to each other bear out the warmth of their own friendship:

Byron to Hobhouse,

You can't conceive how much I miss you – much more than after your departure from Greece. Here there are so many things that we should laugh at together and support each other when laughed at ourselves that I yearn for you prodigiously.

Byron to Hobhouse,

Now I would wish to set apart £3,000 for the tour – do you think *that* would enable me to see all Italy in a gentlemanly way? – with as few servants and luggage – as we can help. – And will you come with me? – you are the only man with whom I could travel an hour ... in short you know my dear H – that with all my bad qualities – and d-d bad they are to be sure – I like you better than any body – and we have travelled together before – and been old friends and all that ... now don't engage yourself – but take up your map – and ponder upon this – ever, dear Hobhouse, your most affectionate   Byron.

After his exile Byron remained a good friend to Hobhouse, encouraging him in his political career without a hint of envy:

Take your fortune – take it at the flood – now is your time and remember that in your very start you have overtaken all whom you thought before you above all don't diffide in yourself – nor be nervous about your health – leave that to poets and such fellows – and don't be afraid of your own talents – I tell you as I have told others – that you think too humbly of yourself ...

Byron defended Sheridan fiercely, looking upon his failings with the most complete understanding and fellow-feeling.

As for his creditors – remember, Sheridan never had a shilling and was thrown, with great powers and passions into the thick of the world, and placed upon the pinnacle of success, with no other external means to support him in his elevation. Did Fox pay his debts? – or did Sheridan take a subscription? Was the Duke of Norfolk's drunkenness more excusable than his? Were his intrigues more notorious than those of all his contemporaries? and is his memory to be blasted and theirs respected? Don't let yourself be led away by clamour, but compare him with the coalitioner, Fox, and the pensioner, Burke, as a man of principle, and with ten hundred thousand in personal views, and with none in talent, for he beat them all out and out. Without means, without connexions, without character (which might be false at first, and make him mad afterwards from desperation) he beat them all in all he ever attempted. But alas poor human nature!

A letter to Hobhouse shows Byron's attitude to friendship:

So – Scrope is gone – down-*diddled* – as Doug K writes it – the said Doug being the Man who when he lost a friend went to the St James's Coffee House and took a new one – but to you and me – the loss of Scrope is irreparable.

Sir Walter Scott wrote of Byron,

What I liked about Byron besides his boundless genius, was his generosity of spirit as well as purse and his utter contempt of all the affectations of literature …

He was devoid of selfishness which I take to be the basest ingredient in the human composition. He was generous, humane and noble minded, when passion did not blind him … I believe much of his affected misanthropy (for I never thought it real) was founded upon instances of ingratitude and selfishness experienced at the hands of those of whom better could not have been expected.

Many and many a pleasant hour have I spent with him and I never met a man with nobler feelings or one who, had he not unfortunately taken the wrong course, might have done more to make himself beloved and respected ... he has had no justice done him.

Everything in his manner, person and conversation tended to maintain the charm which his genius had flung around him and those admitted to his conversation, far from finding that the inspired poet sunk into ordinary mortality, felt themselves attached to him, not only by many noble qualities, but by the interest of a mysterious, undefined, and almost painful curiosity.

The interest which his genius attached to his presence and to his conversation, was of a nature far beyond what his hereditary claims could of themselves have conferred, and his reception was enthusiastic beyond anything we have ever witnessed or heard reported.

Scott thought it a failing in Byron that he tended to foregather with 'indifferent company', by which he meant pugilists, boxers, fencing masters and jockeys. When Angelo and Theodore Hook visited Byron in Cambridge he gave them dinner and saw them off on the coach, sending to St John's for particularly good beer – 'filled two tumblers and handed them up, laughing at the many people wondering at him for waiting on two outside passengers'.

During the time at Missolonghi the boy, Loukas, fell ill. Byron gave up his bed and slept four nights in the common room. When Pietro Gamba was ill the same offer was made to him. During the voyage from Cephalonia, Fletcher came down with a fever and Byron gave him the only mattress on board and slept on deck.

Byron was better disposed towards Shelley than Shelley towards Byron. He wrote to Murray, 'Alas! poor Shelley! – how he would have laughed – had he lived, and how we used to laugh now and then – at various things which are grave in the suburbs.'

His verdict on Shelley was, 'Shelley was truth itself and honour itself, notwithstanding his out-of-the-way notions about religion.'

Why Don't the Scots Claim Byron?

I t is surprising that the Scots lay no very firm claim to Byron who considered himself 'born half a Scot and bred a whole one'. The influence of that Scottish upbringing was incalculable. The bloodstained history of his proud maternal ancestors, the Gordons of Gight, and the prohibitions and guilt of Scottish Calvinism which darkened his life and his poetry, gave an added dimension to both. A childhood spent in Aberdeen made him a lover of the sea and seafarers and of books and bookmen and helped to make him a lifelong sceptic about religion and about political systems and governments. Political discussion in Aberdeen was European in outlook and was certainly not prejudiced in favour of the English Establishment. The *Aberdeen Journal* was enthusiastic for the French Revolution, and France, the traditional enemy of England, was the traditional ally of Scotland. An intelligent ten-year-old travelling south to take up his English inheritance was likely to question much that English boys would take for granted.

The young man who set out on his travels some years later was not convinced of the superiority of everything English. He wrote from Greece,

> Here I have conversed with French, Germans, Italians, Danes, Greeks, Turks, Americans etc and, without losing sight of my own, I can judge of the countries and manners of others. Where I see the superiority of England (which by the bye we are a good deal mistaken in many things) I am pleased, and where I find her inferior I am at least enlightened.

This admirable attitude remained with him all his life. Although he was tormented at Missolonghi by the unreliability of the Greeks, he made allowances for the effect on the Greek character of years of oppression and prophesied that freedom would work wonders. He admired America and contemplated emigrating to Venezuela.

Scotland was the only country which he castigated unmercifully. When he grew older and wiser he made amends for it.

The cruel review of his first book of verse in the *Edinburgh Review* had a traumatic effect on him, half a Scotsman himself. His reply was *English Bards and Scotch Reviewers* which is full of taunts against Scotsmen, including even Sir Walter Scott.

A much worse diatribe was put into the mouth of the goddess, Minerva, in *The Curse of Minerva*, which castigated Lord Elgin for what Byron regarded as his depradations in Greece. Scotland was described as 'A land of meanness sophistry and mist'.

By 1812 Byron had repented of the 'misplaced anger and indiscriminate acrimony' of *English Bards and Scotch Reviewers* and he suppressed any further editions. He must have repented similarly of *The Curse of Minerva* for he printed only eight copies for private circulation. No authorised edition appeared until after his death.

In 1814 he was invited to write an address for the Caledonian Meeting, for an audience of subscribers to a fund for the support of the children of Scottish servicemen who had fought for Britain. The result was a panegyric so fulsome that one might suspect Byron was making amends for his earlier attacks:

> Where bright claymore and hardihood of hand
> No foe could tame no tyrant could command.

Some years later, from exile, he wrote some more convincing lines:

> As Auld Lang Syne brings Scotland one and all,
> Scotch plaids, Scotch snoods, the blue hills and
>   clear streams,
> All my boy feelings, all my gentler dreams.

By then he was good friends with Walter Scott who had freely forgiven him the critical lines in the satire and had defended Byron when all hands were against him. Byron wrote to Scott from Italy, 'The Gods be with your dreams.'

If Byron had not died in Greece he might eventually have been regarded as more than half a Scotsman. Shortly before he set off on his last journey he wrote to ask whether it might be possible to buy back Gight Castle, his mother's ancestral home, which had been gambled away by his feckless father and bought by the Earls of Aberdeen.

Perhaps Byron was contemplating a possible return from exile. Newstead Abbey had been sold. If Gight Castle had become his home he might well have reverted to the Scots way of speaking he had used as a child. Some said he never lost all trace of it.

A descendant of the Gordons of Gight and the Stuart kings living thirty miles north of Aberdeen in his ancestral castle, speaking as Scotsmen speak and exchanging visits with Abbotsford – such a poet would undoubtedly have been claimed by Scotland along with Scott and Burns.

Byron's Animals

The reason why some tyrannical characters have been fond of animals and humane to them is because they have no exercise of reason and could not condemn the wickedness of their master.

Lady Byron

At the heart of the flamboyance lay something cold and hard. One term he arrived back at Cambridge with a bear, got bored with it quickly and never bothered to ask why it died.

Kathryn Hughes, *Daily Telegraph*, 1997

Phyllis Grosskurth agrees with the writers quoted above, claiming that Byron derived reassurance that he was lord of the manor from dependent animals which could be disposed of more easily than human beings.

The evidence is against all three.

Byron brought the bear to Cambridge to annoy the Fellows who would not allow him to keep a dog. Since there was no mention in the Statutes of bears there could be no legal reason for banning the bear. Far from neglecting the bear Byron took it home to Newstead Abbey and when he left for his tour of Europe he asked his unfortunate mother to take care of it. This she undoubtedly did as she took care of the Abbey and the servants and the tenants, but the bear died before Byron returned.

Doris Langley Moore, in her study of Byron's financial affairs, *Lord Byron: Accounts Rendered*, produced carefully re-searched lists of household accounts from which we learn that during his stay in Pisa large amounts of hay, corn, brown oatmeal, beans and honey were purchased for the upkeep of his horses. Byron believed that honey was extremely good for both horses and humans. He used to dose his servants with it and ordered his grooms to add large amounts of honey to the bran mash. The upkeep of the animals at Pisa cost far more than was spent on food for Byron (excluding wine and the lavish dinner parties he gave for the Shelleys, Medwin and others).

One of the few things Byron deplored about his wife was her indifference to the welfare of her servants and her horses. She overworked the horses. Byron once wrote to a friend in his 'hot youth', 'Desire Drury – if he loves me – to kick Dwyer thrice for frightening my horses ... last July.' Byron always kept dogs. The wolf-dog, Lyon, which he left at Newstead with the bear, cost twenty pounds a year. The keep and maintenance of a parlourmaid cost thirty pounds a year.

Byron often wrote about his dogs to his friends.

> Savage ought to be immortal, though not a *thorough bred* bulldog he is the first puppy I ever saw and will answer much better – in his great and manifold kindness he has already bitten my fingers and disturbed the gravity of old Boatswain who is *grievously discomposed*, I wish to be informed of what he cost, his expenses etc. that I may indemnify Mr G.

His favourite dog was Boatswain, a Newfoundland whose picture may be seen at Newstead Abbey. He wrote to Francis Hodgson in 1911,

> Boatswain is dead! He expired in a state of madness on the 10th after suffering much, yet retaining all the gentleness of his nature till the last, never attempting to do the least injury to anyone near him. – I have lost everything – except Old Murray.

(Murray was the butler he had inherited with the Abbey at the age of ten. He loved him dearly.)

Thomas Moore describes how Byron wiped the slaver from the lips of the dying Boatswain.

Boatswain was buried in a vault in the gardens at Newstead. Byron, aged twenty, desired to be buried in the same vault beside the dog. He wrote this epitaph:

Near this spot
Are deposited the Remains of one
Who possessed Beauty without Vanity,
Strength without Insolence,
Courage without Ferocity,
And all the virtues of Man without his Vices.
This Praise, which would be unmeaning Flattery
If inscribed over human ashes,
Is but a just tribute to the Memory of Boatswain,
a Dog.

In 1819 Byron wrote from Italy to Hodgson, 'Fletcher is well – I have got two monkeys and a fox – and two new mastiffs – Mutz is still in high old age. The monkeys are charming.'

In 1820 he wrote to Augusta Leigh, 'How is all your rabbit warren of a family? ... The child Allegra is well – but the monkey has got a cough – and the tame crow has lately suffered from a headache. Fletcher has been bled for a Stitch and looks flourishing again.' This emphasis on the health of his household is no doubt a dig at Augusta who tended to write to him about megrims and earaches instead of the love letters he had earlier longed for.

After Byron's death his friend Kinnaird, who acted as his banker in London, was astonished at receiving a letter from Mr Barry, Byron's banker in Genoa, revealing to him the existence of three tame geese which Byron had left in his care on leaving for Greece. They had been fattening up for Michaelmas and Byron had decided to rescue them from the pot and keep them as pets. They had travelled from Pisa to Genoa swinging in a basket from the Napoleonic coach. Mr Barry proposed sending them to Kinnaird in London.

When the *Florida* arrived from Greece bringing Byron's body home to England with his sorrowful household on board Hobhouse took a boat up-river to board the ship and receive the body. He shed tears at the familiar sight of Byron's three dogs playing on deck.

Books Referred to in the Text

Byron's Letters and Journals, 12 volumes. Edited by Leslie A Marchand. London: John Murray, 1973-82.

The Complete Poetical Works of Byron. Edited by Jerome J McGann. Oxford: Clarendon Press, 1980-1993.

Byron: A Biography, 3 volumes. Leslie A Marchand. London: John Murray, 1958.

The Late Lord Byron. Doris Langley Moore. London: John Murray, 1961.

Lord Byron: Accounts Rendered. Doris Langley Moore. London: John Murray, 1974.

Lord Byron's Wife. Malcolm Elwin. London: Macdonald, 1962.

My Recollections of Lord Byron, 2 volumes. Teresa Giuccioli. London, 1869.

Byron and Shakespeare. G. Wilson Knight. London: Routledge, 1967.

Byron's Don Juan. Bernard Beatty. Beckenham: Croom Helm, 1985.

Byron: Don Juan. Anne Barton. Cambridge: Cambridge University Press, 1992.

Byron and the Limits of Fiction. Edited by Bernard Beatty and Vincent Newey. Liverpool: Liverpool University Press, 1988.

His Very Self and Voice: Collected Conversations of Lord Byron. Edited by Ernest J. Lovell, Jr. New York: Macmillan, 1954.

The Politics of Paradise A Vindication of Byron. Michael Foot. London: Collins, 1988.

Byron and Greek Love. Louis Crompton. London: Faber and Faber, 1985.

The Clairmont Correspondence, 2 volumes. Edited by Marion Kingston Stocking. Baltimore, Johns Hopkins University Press, 1995.

Recollections of a Long Life, 3 volumes. Lord Broughton [John Cam Hobhouse]. London: John Murray, 1981.

The Last Days of Lord Byron. William Parry. London, 1825.

The Blind Man Traces the Circle. Michael Cook. Princeton: Princeton University Press, 1968.

Byron: A Critical Study. Andrew Rutherford. London and Edinburgh: Oliver and Boyd, 1961.

The Two Duchesses. Edited by Vere Foster. London: Blackie and Son, 1898.

Acknowledgements

I am grateful to *The Byron Journal, The Tablet,* and the Parliamentary Weekly: *The House Magazine,* for permission to use material from book reviews of mine which have appeared in those publications.

I am extremely grateful to John Murray for generous permission to quote throughout this little book from *Byron's Letters and Journals* and to John Murray, Collins, Croom Helm, Cambridge University Press, Macmillan, Johns Hopkins University Press and Princeton University Press for the use of brief quotations from books mentioned in the text as listed on pp.59,60.

I am most grateful to Peter Thorogood for permission to use on the cover a wood engraving by George Cruickshank which is reproduced from *The Men in The Moon* by William Hone.

City of Nottingham Museums: Newstead Abbey, have kindly given permission for the reproduction of Byron on p.5.

I would like to thank Bernard Beatty for suggestions and advice given, as always, with the greatest kindness and generosity.

Books by Anne Fleming

Bright Darkness: The Poetry of Lord Byron Presented in the Context of his Life and Times. Nottingham Court Press 1984

In Search of Byron in England and Scotland. Old Forge Press 1988

There Goes Charlie: A Rural Murder. Collins Crime Club 1990

Sophie is Gone. Robert Hale 1994

Death and Deconstruction. Robert Hale 1995

The Desert and the Marketplace: Writings, letters, journals of Ursula Fleming, ed A Fleming. Gracewing 1995

This Means Mischief. Robert Hale 1996

Relaxation for Concentration Stress Management and Pain Control Using the Fleming Method. Butterworth-Heinemann 1997. Joint ed. and compiler A Fleming